CHURCH CHUCKLES

by DICK HAFER

New Leaf Press

First printing: October 1995
Second printing: April 1996

ISBN: 0-89221-304-3
Library of Congress Catalog: 95-71123

Please feel free to use these pages for your bulletins, fax messages, etc.

Dedication

Many thanks to all of my fellow church members
who wrote this book with their lives . . .
while I watched and sketched.

If you don't recognize yourself, watch my future books.
I visit a lot of churches — and I carry my pen.

These cartoons are not meant to make fun
of God's _church_ but to get us to laugh with each other
at the ways of God's _people_ . . . us.

The most effective ministers I've ever known
all shared a vibrant sense of humor.

After all, who has more to be happy about than us?
I've read the back of the book . . . we win!

Laughter is the most beautiful and beneficial therapy God ever granted. — Charles R. Swindoll

Laughing is the sensation of feeling good all over and showing it principally in one spot. — Josh Billings (1818-1885)

FOR CRYIN' OUT LOUD, MOSES!! FOR 40 YEARS YOU'VE HAD THE MAP *UPSIDE DOWN?!!*

NOW HERE'S THE PART YOU'LL LIKE ... ON THE SIXTH DAY,
THE **ANIMALS** WERE CREATED!

IT WORKS!! *I'LL NEVER LOSE SUPPLIES AGAIN!*

THE FIRST THING YOU NEED TO REALIZE IS THAT, LIKE ALL CHURCHES, WE HAVE OUR OWN UNIQUE TRADITIONS.

IF ANYONE KNOWS ANY REASON WHY THESE TWO SHOULD NOT....

BOY, PASTOR WILSON, THIS IS A NEAT IDEA YOU HAD ABOUT AN ALL-NIGHT
NEW YEAR'S EVE GAME AND PARTY NIGHT FOR THE TEENS! IT'S ALMOST 2:30...
WHAT'LL WE DO NEXT, PASTOR WILSON? ... PASTOR WILSON?

IF I TOLD YOU ONCE, I TOLD YOU A THOUSAND TIMES, MOM... "MAKE SURE NOTHING ELSE IS PLANNED FOR THE CHURCH HALL DURING MY RECEPTION!"

18

REALLY? YOU'RE A MINISTER?!! BOY! THIS ALTITUDE IS DOING SOMETHING TO MY HEAD ... I'M TALKIN' FUNNY ... USING WORDS I **NEVER** USE! ISN'T THAT WEIRD?! OH RATS! LOOK AT THIS ... THE STEWARDESS LEFT A ... WHAT DO YOU CALL IT? A **MIXED DRINK** ON MY TRAY!! AND I ASKED FOR MY OLD STANDBY — GINGER ALE ... BOY-O-BOY!

IT FINALLY HAPPENED... 73 JELLO SALADS... AND I PLATE OF CHICKEN!

THAT'S A VERY NICE IDEA, ROY, BUT I DON'T THINK WE CAN AFFORD TO ADVERTISE THE CHURCH BAZAAR ON THE "TONIGHT SHOW."

SOMEHOW I LIKED THE ELECTRONIC CHURCH BETTER BEFORE HOLOGRAMS.

THE EARLY CHURCH IN AMERICA

AMERICA'S FIRST RADIO EVANGELIST.

YES, MRS. BAUMGARTNER . . . I **DO** ENJOY OUR COUNSELING SESSIONS,
BUT ONCE IN A WHILE I DO NEED A DAY OFF TO RELAX.

MRS. HANSEN IS UPSET BECAUSE DURING YOUR SERMON YOU DIDN'T MENTION HER LIVER & NOODLE CASSEROLE FROM LAST SATURDAY'S POTLUCK DINNER.

HERE!! . . . I'VE ALWAYS HATED THIS OUTFIT ON YOU, DON!

26

I SAID **NO STARCH** IN THE ROBES!!

LET ME GET THIS STRAIGHT . . . YOU'RE BAKING ALL OF THIS NEAT STUFF FOR THE CHURCH BAKE SALE, TO RAISE MONEY FOR STARVING CHILDREN OVERSEAS . . . RIGHT? HAVE YOU EVER NOTICED ANY HUNGRY KIDS IN YOUR OWN KITCHEN?

BUT YOU **SAID** WE SHOULD BRING OUR BEST FRIEND TO SUNDAY SCHOOL!

THERE ARE PLENTY OF SEATS FARTHER UP FRONT.

I HOPE IT'S THE FIRST DAY OF STANDARD TIME . . . OTHERWISE
WE MAY HAVE MISSED THE RAPTURE.

HI. I'M BERNIE, A VOLUNTEER WITH YOUR "MEALS ON WHEELS" TEAM. I'M AFRAID I DROPPED YOUR DINNER.... SO I GOT YOU A SPICY BURRITO, HALF OF A PEPPER STEAK SUB, A COLA, AND A CHEWY NUT CANDY BAR.

SO, I FIGURED IT WAS KIND OF A WASTE GOING TO ALL OF THOSE "MOTHER-DAUGHTER" BANQUETS OVER THE YEARS. . . .

JAPHETH! SHEM! MOVE THE HIPPOS AND ELEPHANTS TO THE FRONT!!

NOW *THAT'S* SINGING!!

JENKINTOWN BIBLE CHURCH'S PUPPET MINISTRY.

38

YEAH, EIGHT BUCKS *IS A LOT FOR A MOVIE TICKET,*
BUT HEY — IT'S SUPPOSED TO BE A GOOD FLICK!

BOY! WAS I LUCKY TO GET THESE PLAY-OFF TICKETS
FOR ONLY $55 EACH! **GO, REDSKINS!!**

WHAT A BREAK! ONLY $12 TO PARK
AND IT SAVES US A TWO-BLOCK WALK!

WHAT DO YOU WANT FROM ME?!! I PUT
A WHOLE BUCK IN THE PLATE!!

HELLO THERE. I'M MRS. HANSEN FROM THE HELPING-HAND COMMITTEE AT CHURCH. DON'T YOU WORRY ABOUT A THING WITH YOUR POOR WIFE JUST HOME FROM AN OPERATION. I'VE BROUGHT YOU A GREAT BIG POT OF MY LIVER AND NOODLE CASSEROLE... ENOUGH FOR SEVERAL DELICIOUS MEALS! NO, DON'T THANK ME... YOUR ENJOYMENT IS THANKS ENOUGH!

THE NIGHT THE PASTORAL STAFF LEARNED THAT IT'S RISKY TO PLAY BIBLICAL TRIVIA WITH TWELVE-YEAR-OLD DIANE.

GOD LOVES A CHEERFUL GIVER.

42

THE FELLOWSHIP HALL PAINT-SELECTION COMMITTEE REACHES AN IMPASSE.

LET'S SEE... THIS NUMBER THREE FELLOW ON YOUR LIST, "SAUL OF TARSUS"... HE'S A ROMAN CITIZEN... HE HEADED THE GROUP THAT HUNTED DOWN AND KILLED MANY OF OUR FELLOW BELIEVERS... HE STONED FOLKS... SENT LOADS OF US TO PRISON. NATHAN, WE'VE HAD SOME LOUSY CALL COMMITTEE CHAIRMEN IN THE PAST, **BUT YOU TAKE THE CAKE!!!**

AND WE FURTHER DEMAND THAT YOU CHANGE *THAT* TO *"HERS"* ON ALTERNATE SUNDAYS!

WE NEED COUNSELING, PASTOR. POOPSIE SAYS I'M TOO AGGRESSIVE WITH HER.

I'M **NOT** AN OLD FOGEY! I JUST KINDA LIKED THE TRADITIONAL LITURGY!

BUT LET ME NOT BELABOR THE POINT.

ED HERE IS OUR POTLUCK PRO.

HIGH-TECH CHURCH MEETING TIMESAVERS.

I THINK WE NEED TO TALK ABOUT THE MEANING OF BAPTISM, GLENN.

YEAH. IT'S BEEN THIS WAY EVER SINCE HE WENT TO
A JERRY FALWELL PREACHER'S CONFERENCE.

WHY DIDN'T YOU TELL US THAT THE WOMEN'S RETREAT WAS AT A **SCOUT** CAMP!!!

IT'S BEEN SO NICE HAVING YOU FOR DINNER, VICAR STEVENS. I LOVE TO WATCH A HUNGRY YOUNG MAN EAT MY MEALS! LAND SAKES . . . YOU CLEANED UP EVERY PLATE OF MY LIVER AND NOODLE CASSEROLE THAT I DISHED OUT FOR YOU!

MILDRED, WE **KNOW** YOU'VE PLAYED MARY IN THE CHRISTMAS PAGEANT FOR 23 YEARS, AND WE **DO** APPRECIATE IT . . . BUT. . . .

THERE'S BEEN AN ACCIDENT!!

THEREFORE, LET HE WHO IS WITHOUT SIN CAST THE FIRST STONE.

WHY THE CHURCH JANITOR DREADS "YOUTH GROUP TAFFY NIGHT."

62

GOOD MORNING! I'M PROFESSOR STEINBACH AND I'M A NEW MEMBER OF YOUR CLASS. I TEACH SYSTEMATIC THEOLOGY AND ESCHATOLOGY AT THE SEMINARY.

NOW, NOW, CHILDREN . . . WE MUSTN'T BOTHER MR. TAYLOR
WHILE HE'S TUNING THE PIANO.

OF **COURSE** I'M GOING TO HEAVEN!! GRANDPAPA **FOUNDED** THIS CHURCH!

WE GOT PLENTY OF PANCAKES... BUT WHERE ARE ALL THE **SAUSAGES?**

I DUNNO... I'M INCLINED TO VOTE "NO" ON THIS MEMBERSHIP APPLICATION, BECAUSE HE DIDN'T GIVE A VERY CLEAR TESTIMONY; ON THE OTHER HAND, HE **DOES** HAVE A BEACH HOUSE AND A BOAT. ...

WALTER . . . I DON'T THINK THAT'S WHAT
JIM KENNEDY MEANT BY "EVANGELISM EXPLOSION."

70

AND THE WINNER OF THE ATTENDANCE AWARD IS MORTON RANDEL, WHO HASN'T MISSED A SUNDAY SCHOOL CLASS SINCE 1973! HE WINS ONE OF MRS. HANSEN'S FAMOUS LIVER AND NOODLE CASSEROLE DINNERS, AT HER HOUSE.

HAW! HAW! YOU'RE GONNA NEED MORE THAN PRAYER ON THIS **HOLE**, PASTOR!

IF THAT DON'T BEAT ALL!! THREE POUNDS OF COOKIES AND A GALLON OF MILK GONE!
WHAT ARE WE GONNA SERVE TO BEGINNER'S CLASS NOW? WHO WOULD DO THAT?!!

YOU'LL NEVER KNOW HOW MUCH IT WARMS MY HEART TO SEE YOU COME FORWARD!

I HELPED OUT! I WENT THROUGH MOM'S CUPBOARD AND BROUGHT OUR GREEN BEANS, SUCCOTASH, SAUERKRAUT, ASPARAGUS, BROCCOLI, AND SPINACH! **THIS IS A GREAT IDEA!!**

HOLD IT RIGHT THERE!... YOU'RE NOT SUPPOSED TO HAVE FUN IN CHURCH!!

YOU OUGHT TO GO TO THE CHURCH YOUTH GROUP, DEAR. YOU MIGHT MEET SOME NICE YOUNG MAN. HE MIGHT EVEN DATE YOU. . . . YOU NEVER KNOW WHERE THAT MIGHT LEAD. IF HE COMES FROM A NICE FAMILY, YOU MIGHT EVEN GET ENGAGED . . . MAYBE EVEN MARRIED . . . AND HAVE KIDS . . . AND IF YOU THINK I'M GONNA SIT WITH ALL THOSE KIDS EVERY DAY, **YOU'VE GOT ANOTHER THINK COMING, YOUNG LADY!**

I FOUND ONE!! _HE DOESN'T HAVE A "KING JAMES - 1611"!!_

IT'S SHAMEFUL, PASTOR! YOU WOULDN'T BELIEVE WHAT GOES ON BEHIND DEACON SIMPSON'S NEARLY CLOSED WINDOWS! . . . NOT TO MENTION WHAT THEY KEEP IN THEIR DRAWERS AND AT THE BACK OF THEIR CLOSET!! LAND SAKES ALIVE!

SO, I WANT TO SAY HOW MUCH I APPRECIATE THOSE OF YOU WHO ARE HERE TONIGHT, EVEN THOUGH SOME BACKSLIDERS STAYED HOME TO WATCH THE SUPER BOWL.

ME WORK IN THE NURSERY?!! NO WAY! I GOT 'EM ALL WEEK!

YEAH . . . HE'S GOT LOTS OF GUTS ALL RIGHT.

THE YOUTH PASTOR HAS HEARD THE RUMORS THAT HE LOOKS TOO YOUNG.

MR. WHARTON IS **SO** SPIRITUAL. HE EVEN COMES TO SUNDAY SCHOOL
ON DAYS WE DON'T HAVE DOUGHNUTS!

NO!! MRS. HANSEN DONATED MORE OF HER LIVER & NOODLE CASSEROLE! HAVEN'T THOSE POOR FLOOD VICTIMS SUFFERED ENOUGH?!!

SORRY!... MARIE FORGOT TO RUN THE BULLETIN YESTERDAY!

YOU'RE RIGHT!... YOU'VE FINALLY CONVINCED ME!...
OLD PASTOR SURRATT **WAS** BETTER THAN I AM!... HERE, GO DIG HIM UP!!

THE GOOD NEWS IS THAT THE NEW CROSS LOOKS REAL NICE
ON TOP OF THE STEEPLE. THANKS, FRED.

WE'VE **GOT** TO DO SOMETHING ABOUT ENLARGING THE CHURCH!

OH, BE STILL MY HEART! JOY IS ME! I'VE GOT A RELIGIOUS TRACT FOR A TIP!

I DON'T THINK THEY GET MANY VISITORS.

IS THAT RIGHT, DEACON HARMON? FIRST DAY OF
DAYLIGHT SAVING TIME? HOW ABOUT THAT?

ALL RIGHT! . . . NO SNACK BAR PRIVILEGES UNTIL YOU GIVE BACK COUNSELOR ELLIS!!

YES, BEING A MISSIONARY IN THE BUSH COUNTRY **CAN** BE HAZARDOUS. WHY DO YOU ASK?

CRAIG REALLY THROWS HIMSELF INTO HIS CHALK-TALKS!

I BET BILLY GRAHAM ATE HIS BROCCOLI FOR **HIS** MOTHER!

ER...AH...ASIDE FROM **THAT**, DO YOU AND YOUR WIFE HAVE ANY OTHER HOBBIES?

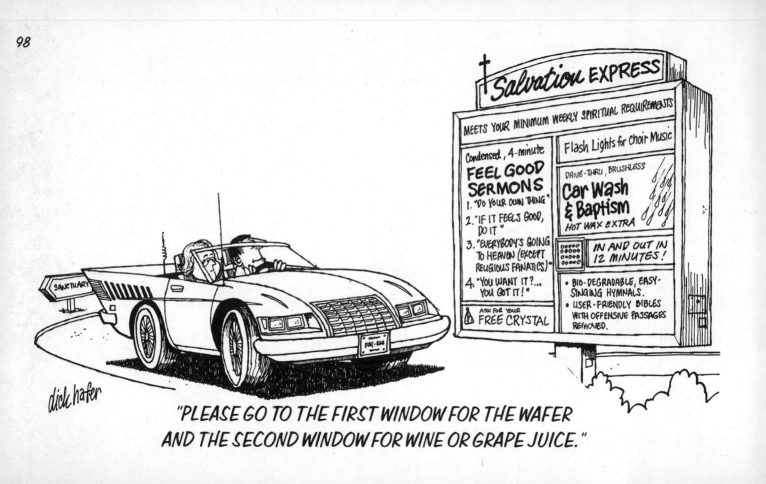

"PLEASE GO TO THE FIRST WINDOW FOR THE WAFER AND THE SECOND WINDOW FOR WINE OR GRAPE JUICE."

IT'LL NEVER FLY A FEW THOUSAND YEARS FROM NOW. . . .
HE DON'T LOOK **ANYTHING** LIKE CHARLTON HESTON!

NO, NO, MRS. HANSEN! YOU JUST RELAX AND I'LL GET YOUR DISH!
ONCE AGAIN, YOUR LIVER & NOODLE CASSEROLE WAS THE HIT OF THE POTLUCK DINNER!

HOW COME HE DIDN'T SHOW UP THE SUNDAY I WAS HERE TO SEE HIM? DADDY SAYS "MR. SANDMAN" ALWAYS VISITS THE CHURCH WHEN **YOU** PREACH!

WE **WERE** CAMPING IN THE BACK YARD . . . BUT WE HEARD A NOISE.

"THIS IS PASTOR KENDALL. I'M OUT ON CALLS THIS EVENING. IF YOU WANT TO LEAVE A MESSAGE, GIVE YOUR NAME AND PHONE NUMBER AFTER THE BEEP." **"BEEP!"**

MAN!! . . . THAT WAS *SOME SERMON!!*

I DON'T WANT TO SOUND UNGRATEFUL, BUT WHEN THE SIMPSONS SAID THEY WERE GOING TO DONATE A SWIMMING POOL TO THE YOUTH GROUP, I THOUGHT....

dich hafer

BENNY!! *IT'S ONLY A CHURCH PICNIC GAME!!*

I HEARD THAT, LADY!! THIS IS NOT THE WAY HELL WILL LOOK!!

YEAH... PASTOR NIETING'S A MODEL RAILROAD BUFF.

IRENE FINDS IT DISCOURAGING TO WITNESS AT THE MALL.

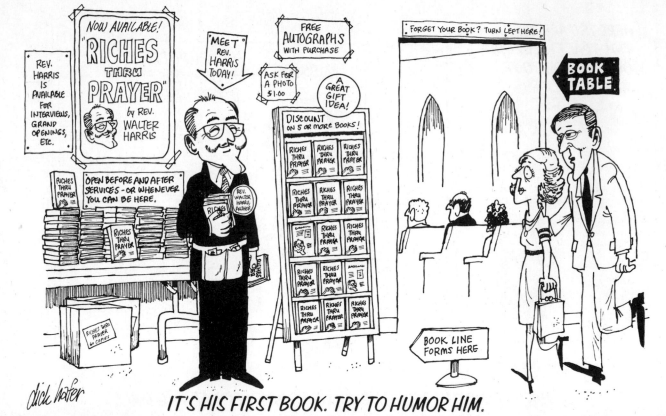

IT'S HIS FIRST BOOK. TRY TO HUMOR HIM.

YEAH... THE BUILDING COMMITTEE NEVER COULD GET TOGETHER ON AN ARCHITECTURAL STYLE FOR THE NEW CHURCH.

WOW! THIS IS THE BEST MEAL WE'VE HAD IN THREE WEEKS, NOAH!!

WE'RE WATCHING FOR THE RAPTURE! WANNA JOIN US?

ISN'T BIBLE STUDY AT **OUR** HOUSE **NEXT** FRIDAY?!!

YEAH ... BILL JONES IS A NATURAL-BORN SUNDAY SCHOOL TEACHER!

FOR CRYIN' OUT LOUD!! *THE ENTIRE CHURCH FREEZER IS STUFFED WITH MRS. HANSEN'S LIVER & NOODLE CASSEROLE!!*

WHAT'S THE MATTER, JONAH? YOU ALWAYS **LOVED** FISH!

YOU'VE JUST GOT TO COME OVER AND VISIT WITH US. MY, YOU'RE A FINE YOUNG YOUTH PASTOR! YOU'VE GOT TO MEET MY BEAUTIFUL, SPIRITUAL, INTELLIGENT, **SINGLE** DAUGHTER, JENNIFER!

MAYBE WE SHOULD HAVE APPLIED FOR A LESS DANGEROUS
MISSION STATION... RATHER THAN HERE IN NEWARK!

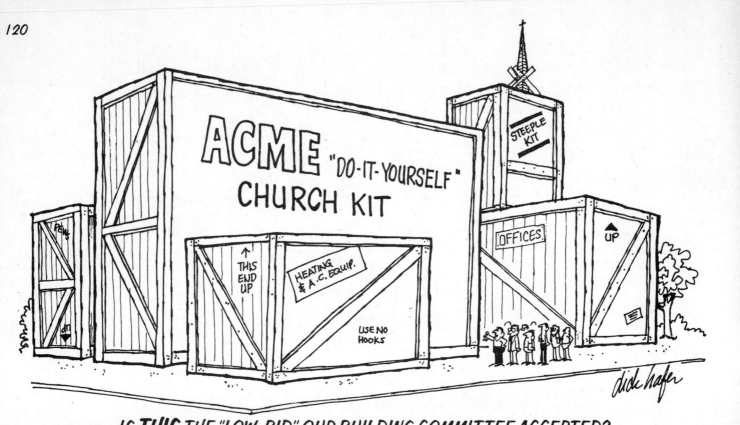

IS **THIS** THE "LOW-BID" OUR BUILDING COMMITTEE ACCEPTED?

I'LL GO VISIT THE SICK TOMORROW! I'M BUSY EVANGELIZING ON THE INTERNET!

SOMEHOW A "LIVING CHRISTMAS TREE" WORKS BETTER IN A BIG CHURCH.

WHEN DONNA REALIZED IT ISN'T ALWAYS A GOOD IDEA TO TIE YOUR PRIMARY
SUNDAY SCHOOL STUDENTS TOGETHER WHILE ON A FIELD TRIP.

I SEE DIANE ARRIVED.

RECIPE FOR "MRS. HANSEN'S LIVER & NOODLE CASSEROLE"

We have received many requests, and even demands, concerning this recipe . . . but we decided to include it anyway. Her specialty has become notorious at potluck dinners throughout the land.

2-1/4 gal. - medium egg noodles	1 tbsp. - salt	3 cups - onion, finely chopped
6 lbs. - chicken livers	2 tbsp. - curry powder	2-1/4 cups - margarine, stick
3 lbs. - fresh mushrooms	1 tbsp. - Old Bay seasoning	3 cups - whole milk
6 cans - cream of mushroom soup	3 cups - celery, finely chopped	1 tsp. - black pepper

Cook noodles according to package instructions. Drain. Use a spray (Pam or equivalent) on the inside of the casserole(s). Pan fry all other ingredients in melted margarine. Add all ingredients together in the cooking container(s). Crush a layer of corn flakes on top of mixture for texture, taste, and looks. Cook 35 - 40 minutes at 350 degrees.

SERVINGS: This recipe will serve 50 at a church dinner (or an infinite number, really — since it's unlikely anyone will touch it).

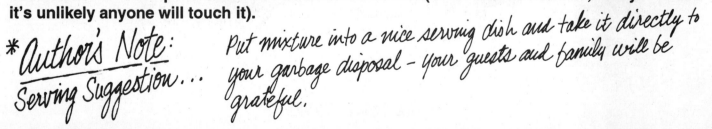

Author's Note: Serving Suggestion...

Put mixture into a nice serving dish and take it directly to your garbage disposal — your guests and family will be grateful.

Also available . . .

MORE **CHURCH CHUCKLES**
by **DICK HAFER**

SUNDAY SCHOOL PATROL

"We had 1,786 in Sunday school last week"